Love-Songs of Childhood by Eugene Field

Eugene Field was born on 2nd September 1850 in St. Louis, Missouri. His mother died when he was six and his father when he was nineteen. His academic life was not taken seriously and he preferred the life of a prankster until, in 1875, he began work as a journalist for the St. Joseph Gazette in Saint Joseph, Missouri.

In his career as a journalist he soon found a niche that suited him. His articles were light, humorous and written in a personal gossipy style that endeared him to his readership. Some were soon being syndicated to other newspapers around the States. Field soon rose to city editor of the Gazette.

Field had first published poetry in 1879, when his poem 'Christmas Treasures' appeared. This was the beginning that would eventually number over a dozen volumes. As well as verse Field published an extensive range of short stories including 'The Holy Cross' and 'Daniel and the Devil.'

In 1889 whilst the family were in London and Field himself was recovering from a bout of ill health he wrote his most famous poem; 'Lovers Lane'.

On 4th November 1895 Eugene Field Sr died in Chicago of a heart attack at the age of 45.

Index of Contents

DEDICATION: To Mrs. Belle Angler

Dearest Aunt:

Many years ago you used to rock me to sleep, cradling me in your arms and singing me petty songs. Surely you have not forgotten that time, and I recall it with tenderness. You were very beautiful then. But you are more beautiful now; for, in the years that have come and gone since then, the joys and the sorrows of maternity have impressed their saintly grace upon the dear face I used to kiss, and have made your gentle heart gentler still.

Beloved lady, in memory of years to be recalled only in thought, and in token of my gratitude and affection, I bring you these little love-songs, and reverently I lay them at your feet.

THE ROCK-A-BY LADY

The Rock-a-By Lady from Hushaby street
Comes stealing; comes creeping;
The poppies they hang from her head to her feet,
And each hath a dream that is tiny and fleet—
She bringeth her poppies to you, my sweet,
When she findeth you sleeping!

There is one little dream of a beautiful drum—
"Rub-a-dub!" it goeth;
There is one little dream of a big sugar-plum,
And lo! thick and fast the other dreams come
Of popguns that bang, and tin tops that hum,
And a trumpet that bloweth!

And dollies peep out of those wee little dreams
With laughter and singing;
And boats go a-floating on silvery streams,
And the stars peek-a-boo with their own misty gleams,
And up, up, and up, where the Mother Moon beams,
The fairies go winging!

Would you dream all these dreams that are tiny and fleet?
They'll come to you sleeping;
So shut the two eyes that are weary, my sweet,
For the Rock-a-By Lady from Hushaby street,
With poppies that hang from her head to her feet,
Comes stealing; comes creeping.

"BOOH!"

On afternoons, when baby boy has had a splendid nap,
And sits, like any monarch on his throne, in nurse's lap,
In some such wise my handkerchief I hold before my face,
And cautiously and quietly I move about the place;
Then, with a cry, I suddenly expose my face to view,
And you should hear him laugh and crow when I say "Booh"!

Sometimes the rascal tries to make believe that he is scared,
And really, when I first began, he stared, and stared, and stared;
And then his under lip came out and farther out it came,
Till mamma and the nurse agreed it was a "cruel shame"—
But now what does that same wee, toddling, lisping baby do
But laugh and kick his little heels when I say "Booh!"

He laughs and kicks his little heels in rapturous glee, and then
In shrill, despotic treble bids me "do it all aden!"
And I—of course I do it; for, as his progenitor,
It is such pretty, pleasant play as this that I am for!
And it is, oh, such fun I am sure that we shall rue
The time when we are both too old to play the game "Booh!"

GARDEN AND CRADLE

When our babe he goeth walking in his garden,
Around his tinkling feet the sunbeams play;
The posies they are good to him,
And bow them as they should to him,
As fareth he upon his kingly way;
And birdlings of the wood to him
Make music, gentle music, all the day,

When our babe he goeth walking in his garden.

When our babe he goeth swinging in his cradle,
Then the night it looketh ever sweetly down;
The little stars are kind to him,
The moon she hath a mind to him
And layeth on his head a golden crown;
And singeth then the wind to him
A song, the gentle song of Bethlem-town,
When our babe he goeth swinging in his cradle.

THE NIGHT WIND

Have you ever heard the wind go "Yooooo"?
'T is a pitiful sound to hear!
It seems to chill you through and through
With a strange and speechless fear.
'T is the voice of the night that broods outside
When folk should be asleep,
And many and many's the time I've cried
To the darkness brooding far and wide
Over the land and the deep:
"Whom do you want, O lonely night,
That you wail the long hours through?"
And the night would say in its ghostly way:
"Yoooooooo!
Yoooooooo!
Yoooooooo!"

My mother told me long ago
(When I was a little tad)
That when the night went wailing so,
Somebody had been bad;
And then, when I was snug in bed,
Whither I had been sent,
With the blankets pulled up round my head,
I'd think of what my mother'd said,
And wonder what boy she meant!
And "Who's been bad to-day?" I'd ask
Of the wind that hoarsely blew,
And the voice would say in its meaningful way:
"Yoooooooo!
Yoooooooo!
Yoooooooo!"

That this was true I must allow—
You'll not believe it, though!
Yes, though I'm quite a model now,
I was not always so.

And if you doubt what things I say,
Suppose you make the test;
Suppose, when you've been bad some day
And up to bed are sent away
From mother and the rest—
Suppose you ask, "Who has been bad?"
And then you'll hear what's true;
For the wind will moan in its ruefulest tone:
"Yoooooooo!
Yoooooooo!
Yoooooooo!"

KISSING TIME

'T is when the lark goes soaring
And the bee is at the bud,
When lightly dancing zephyrs
Sing over field and flood;
When all sweet things in nature
Seem joyfully achime—
'T is then I wake my darling,
For it is kissing time!

Go, pretty lark, a-soaring,
And suck your sweets, O bee;
Sing, O ye winds of summer,
Your songs to mine and me;
For with your song and rapture
Cometh the moment when
It's half-past kissing time
And time to kiss again!

So—so the days go fleeting
Like golden fancies free,
And every day that cometh
Is full of sweets for me;
And sweetest are those moments
My darling comes to climb
Into my lap to mind me
That it is kissing time.

Sometimes, maybe, he wanders
A heedless, aimless way—
Sometimes, maybe, he loiters
In pretty, prattling play;
But presently bethinks him
And hastens to me then,
For it's half-past kissing time
And time to kiss again!

JEST 'FORE CHRISTMAS

Father calls me William, sister calls me Will,
Mother calls me Willie, but the fellers call me Bill!
Mighty glad I ain't a girl—ruther be a boy,
Without them sashes, curls, an' things that's worn by Fauntleroy!
Love to chawnk green apples an' go swimmin' in the lake—
Hate to take the castor-ile they give for bellyache!
'Most all the time, the whole year round, there ain't no flies on me,
But jest 'fore Christmas I'm as good as I kin be!

Got a yeller dog named Sport, sick him on the cat;
First thing she knows she doesn't know where she is at!
Got a clipper sled, an' when us kids goes out to slide,
'Long comes the grocery cart, an' we all hook a ride!
But sometimes when the grocery man is worrited an' cross,
He reaches at us with his whip, an' larrups up his hoss,
An' then I laff an' holler, "Oh, ye never teched me!"
But jest 'fore Christmas I'm as good as I kin be!

Gran'ma says she hopes that when I git to be a man,
I'll be a missionarer like her oldest brother, Dan,
As was et up by the cannibuls that lives in Ceylon's Isle,
Where every prospeck pleases, an' only man is vile!
But gran'ma she has never been to see a Wild West show,
Nor read the Life of Daniel Boone, or else I guess she'd know
That Buff'lo Bill an' cow-boys is good enough for me!
Excep' jest 'fore Christmas, when I'm good as I kin be!

And then old Sport he hangs around, so solemn-like an' still,
His eyes they seem a-sayin': "What's the matter, little Bill?"
The old cat sneaks down off her perch an' wonders what's become
Of them two enemies of hern that used to make things hum!
But I am so perlite an' 'tend so earnestly to biz,
That mother says to father: "How improved our Willie is!"
But father, havin' been a boy hisself, suspicions me
When, jest 'fore Christmas, I'm as good as I kin be!

For Christmas, with its lots an' lots of candies, cakes, an' toys,
Was made, they say, for proper kids an' not for naughty boys;
So wash yer face an' bresh yer hair, an' mind yer p's and q's,
An' don't bust out yer pantaloons, and don't wear out yer shoes;
Say "Yessum" to the ladies, an' "Yessur" to the men,
An' when they's company, don't pass yer plate for pie again;
But, thinkin' of the things yer'd like to see upon that tree,
Jest 'fore Christmas be as good as yer kin be!

BEARD AND BABY

I say, as one who never feared
The wrath of a subscriber's bullet,
I pity him who has a beard
But has no little girl to pull it!

When wife and I have finished tea,
Our baby woos me with her prattle,
And, perching proudly on my knee,
She gives my petted whiskers battle.

With both her hands she tugs away,
While scolding at me kind o' spiteful;
You'll not believe me when I say
I find the torture quite delightful!

No other would presume, I ween,
To trifle with this hirsute wonder,
Else would I rise in vengeful mien
And rend his vandal frame asunder!

But when her baby fingers pull
This glossy, sleek, and silky treasure,
My cup of happiness is full—
I fairly glow with pride and pleasure!

And, sweeter still, through all the day
I seem to hear her winsome prattle—
I seem to feel her hands at play,
As though they gave me sportive battle.

Yes, heavenly music seems to steal
Where thought of her forever lingers,
And round my heart I always feel
The twining of her dimpled fingers!

THE DINKEY BIRD

In an ocean, 'way out yonder
(As all sapient people know),
Is the land of Wonder-Wander,
Whither children love to go;
It's their playing, romping, swinging,
That give great joy to me
While the Dinkey-Bird goes singing
In the amfalula tree!

There the gum-drops grow like cherries,
And taffy's thick as peas—
Caramels you pick like berries
When, and where, and how you please;
Big red sugar-plums are clinging
To the cliffs beside that sea
Where the Dinkey-Bird is singing
In the amfalula tree.

So when children shout and scamper
And make merry all the day,
When there's naught to put a damper
To the ardor of their play;
When I hear their laughter ringing,
Then I'm sure as sure can be
That the Dinkey-Bird is singing
In the amfalula tree.

For the Dinkey-Bird's bravuras
And staccatos are so sweet—
His roulades, appoggiaturas,
And robustos so complete,
That the youth of every nation—
Be they near or far away—
Have especial delectation
In that gladsome roundelay.

Their eyes grow bright and brighter,
Their lungs begin to crow,
Their hearts get light and lighter,
And their cheeks are all aglow;
For an echo cometh bringing
The news to all and me,
That the Dinkey-Bird is singing
In the amfalula tree.

I'm sure you like to go there
To see your feathered friend—
And so many goodies grow there
You would like to comprehend!
Speed, little dreams, your winging
To that land across the sea
Where the Dinkey-Bird is singing
In the amfalula tree!

THE DRUM

I'm a beautiful red, red drum,
And I train with the soldier boys;

As up the street we come,
Wonderful is our noise!
There's Tom, and Jim, and Phil,
And Dick, and Nat, and Fred,
While Widow Cutler's Bill
And I march on ahead,
With a r-r-rat-tat-tat
And a tum-titty-um-tum-tum—
Oh, there's bushels of fun in that
For boys with a little red drum!

The Injuns came last night
While the soldiers were abed,
And they gobbled a Chinese kite
And off to the woods they fled!
The woods are the cherry-trees
Down in the orchard lot,
And the soldiers are marching to seize
The booty the Injuns got.
With tum-titty-um-tum-tum,
And r-r-rat-tat-tat,
When soldiers marching come
Injuns had better scat!

Step up there, little Fred,
And, Charley, have a mind!
Jim is as far ahead
As you two are behind!
Ready with gun and sword
Your valorous work to do—
Yonder the Injun horde
Are lying in wait for you.
And their hearts go pitapat
When they hear the soldiers come
With a r-r-rat-tat-tat
And a tum-titty-um-tum-tum!

Course it's all in play!
The skulking Injun crew
That hustled the kite away
Are little white boys, like you!
But "honest" or "just in fun,"
It is all the same to me;
And, when the battle is won,
Home once again march we
With a r-r-rat-tat-tat
And tum-titty-um-tum-tum;
And there's glory enough in that
For the boys with their little red drum!

THE DEAD BABE

Last night, as my dear babe lay dead,
In agony I knelt and said:
"O God! what have I done,
Or in what wise offended Thee,
That Thou should'st take away from me
My little son?

"Upon the thousand useless lives,
Upon the guilt that vaunting thrives,
Thy wrath were better spent!
Why should'st Thou take my little son—
Why should'st Thou vent Thy wrath upon
This innocent?"

Last night, as my dear babe lay dead,
Before mine eyes the vision spread
Of things that might have been:
Licentious riot, cruel strife,
Forgotten prayers, a wasted life
Dark red with sin!

Then, with sweet music in the air,
I saw another vision there:
A Shepherd in whose keep
A little lamb—my little child!
Of worldly wisdom undefiled,
Lay fast asleep!

Last night, as my dear babe lay dead,
In those two messages I read
A wisdom manifest;
And though my arms be childless now,
I am content—to Him I bow
Who knoweth best.

THE HAPPY HOUSEHOLD

It's when the birds go piping and the daylight slowly breaks,
That, clamoring for his dinner, our precious baby wakes;
Then it's sleep no more for baby, and it's sleep no more for me,
For, when he wants his dinner, why it's dinner it must be!
And of that lacteal fluid he partakes with great ado,
While gran'ma laughs,
And gran'pa laughs,
And wife, she laughs,
And I—well, I laugh, too!

You'd think, to see us carrying on about that little tad,
That, like as not, that baby was the first we'd ever had;
But, sakes alive! he isn't, yet we people make a fuss
As if the only baby in the world had come to us!
And, morning, noon, and night-time, whatever he may do,
Gran'ma, she laughs,
Gran'pa, he laughs,
Wife, she laughs,
And I, of course, laugh, too!

But once—a likely spell ago—when that poor little chick
From teething or from some such ill of infancy fell sick,
You wouldn't know us people as the same that went about
A-feelin' good all over, just to hear him crow and shout;
And, though the doctor poohed our fears and said he'd pull him through,
Old gran'ma cried,
And gran'pa cried,
And wife, she cried,
And I—yes, I cried, too!

It makes us all feel good to have a baby on the place,
With his everlastin' crowing and his dimpling, dumpling face;
The patter of his pinky feet makes music everywhere,
And when he shakes those fists of his, good-by to every care!
No matter what our trouble is, when he begins to coo,
Old gran'ma laughs,
And gran'pa laughs,
Wife, she laughs,
And I—you bet, I laugh, too!

SO, SO, ROCK-A-BY SO!

So, so, rock-a-by so!
Off to the garden where dreamikins grow;
And here is a kiss on your winkyblink eyes,
And here is a kiss on your dimpledown cheek
And here is a kiss for the treasure that lies
In the beautiful garden way up in the skies
Which you seek.
Now mind these three kisses wherever you go—
So, so, rock-a-by so!

There's one little fumfay who lives there, I know,
For he dances all night where the dreamikins grow;
I send him this kiss on your droopydrop eyes,
I send him this kiss on your rosyred cheek.
And here is a kiss for the dream that shall rise
When the fumfay shall dance in those far-away skies

Which you seek.
Be sure that you pay those three kisses you owe—
So, so, rock-a-by so!

And, by-low, as you rock-a-by go,
Don't forget mother who loveth you so!
And here is her kiss on your weepydeep eyes,
And here is her kiss on your peachypink cheek,
And here is her kiss for the dreamland that lies
Like a babe on the breast of those far-away skies
Which you seek—
The blinkywink garden where dreamikins grow—
So, so, rock-a-by so!

THE SONG OF LUDDY-DUD

A sunbeam comes a-creeping
Into my dear one's nest,
And sings to our babe a-sleeping
The song that I love the best:
"'T is little Luddy-Dud in the morning—
'T is little Luddy-Dud at night;
And all day long
'T is the same sweet song
Of that waddling, toddling, coddling little mite,
Luddy-Dud."

The bird to the tossing clover,
The bee to the swaying bud,
Keep singing that sweet song over
Of wee little Luddy-Dud.
"'T is little Luddy-Dud in the morning—
'T is little Luddy-Dud at night;
And all day long
'T is the same dear song
Of that growing, crowing, knowing little sprite,
Luddy-Dud."

Luddy-Dud's cradle is swinging
Where softly the night winds blow,
And Luddy-Dud's mother is singing
A song that is sweet and low:
"'T is little Luddy-Dud in the morning—
'T is little Luddy-Dud at night;
And all day long
'T is the same sweet song
Of my nearest and my dearest heart's delight,
Luddy-Dud!"

THE DUEL

The gingham dog and the calico cat
Side by side on the table sat;
'T was half-past twelve, and (what do you think!)
Nor one nor t' other had slept a wink!
The old Dutch clock and the Chinese plate
Appeared to know as sure as fate
There was going to be a terrible spat.
(I wasn't there; I simply state
What was told to me by the Chinese plate!)

The gingham dog went "bow-wow-wow!"
And the calico cat replied "mee-ow!"
The air was littered, an hour or so,
With bits of gingham and calico,
While the old Dutch clock in the chimney place
Up with its hands before its face,
For it always dreaded a family row!
(Now mind: I'm only telling you
What the old Dutch clock declares is true!)

The Chinese plate looked very blue,
And wailed, "Oh, dear! what shall we do!"
But the gingham dog and the calico cat
Wallowed this way and tumbled that,
Employing every tooth and claw
In the awfullest way you ever saw—
And, oh! how the gingham and calico flew!
(Don't fancy I exaggerate—
I got my news from the Chinese plate!)

Next morning, where the two had sat
They found no trace of dog or cat;
And some folks think unto this day
That burglars stole that pair away!
But the truth about the cat and pup
Is this: they ate each other up!
Now what do you really think of that!
(The old Dutch clock it told me so,
And that is how I came to know.)

GOOD-CHILDREN STREET

There's a dear little home in Good-Children street—
My heart turneth fondly to-day
Where tinkle of tongues and patter of feet

Make sweetest of music at play;
Where the sunshine of love illumines each face
And warms every heart in that old-fashioned place.

For dear little children go romping about
With dollies and tin tops and drums,
And, my! how they frolic and scamper and shout
Till bedtime too speedily comes!
Oh, days they are golden and days they are fleet
With little folk living in Good-Children street.

See, here comes an army with guns painted red,
And swords, caps, and plumes of all sorts;
The captain rides gaily and proudly ahead
On a stick-horse that prances and snorts!
Oh, legions of soldiers you're certain to meet—
Nice make-believe soldiers—in Good-Children street.

And yonder Odette wheels her dolly about—
Poor dolly! I'm sure she is ill,
For one of her blue china eyes has dropped out
And her voice is asthmatic'ly shrill.
Then, too, I observe she is minus her feet,
Which causes much sorrow in Good-Children street.

'T is so the dear children go romping about
With dollies and banners and drums,
And I venture to say they are sadly put out
When an end to their jubilee comes:
Oh, days they are golden and days they are fleet
With little folk living in Good-Children street!

But when falleth night over river and town,
Those little folk vanish from sight,
And an angel all white from the sky cometh down
And guardeth the babes through the night,
And singeth her lullabies tender and sweet
To the dear little people in Good-Children Street.

Though elsewhere the world be o'erburdened with care,
Though poverty fall to my lot,
Though toil and vexation be always my share,
What care I—they trouble me not!
This thought maketh life ever joyous and Sweet:
There's a dear little home in Good-Children street.

THE DELECTABLE BALLAD OF THE WALLER LOT

Up yonder in Buena Park

There is a famous spot,
In legend and in history
Yclept the Waller Lot.

There children play in daytime
And lovers stroll by dark,
For 't is the goodliest trysting-place
In all Buena Park.

Once on a time that beauteous maid,
Sweet little Sissy Knott,
Took out her pretty doll to walk
Within the Waller Lot.

While thus she fared, from Ravenswood
Came Injuns o'er the plain,
And seized upon that beauteous maid
And rent her doll in twain.

Oh, 't was a piteous thing to hear
Her lamentations wild;
She tore her golden curls and cried:
"My child! My child! My child!"

Alas, what cared those Injun chiefs
How bitterly wailed she?
They never had been mothers,
And they could not hope to be!

"Have done with tears," they rudely quoth,
And then they bound her hands;
For they proposed to take her off
To distant border lands.

But, joy! from Mr. Eddy's barn
Doth Willie Clow behold
The sight that makes his hair rise up
And all his blood run cold.

He put his fingers in his mouth
And whistled long and clear,
And presently a goodly horde
Of cow-boys did appear.

Cried Willie Clow: "My comrades bold,
Haste to the Waller Lot,
And rescue from that Injun band
Our charming Sissy Knott!"

"Spare neither Injun buck nor squaw,
But smite them hide and hair!

Spare neither sex nor age nor size,
And no condition spare!"

Then sped that cow-boy band away,
Full of revengeful wrath,
And Kendall Evans rode ahead
Upon a hickory lath.

And next came gallant Dady Field
And Willie's brother Kent,
The Eddy boys and Robbie James,
On murderous purpose bent.

For they were much beholden to
That maid—in sooth, the lot
Were very, very much in love
With charming Sissy Knott.

What wonder? She was beauty's queen,
And good beyond compare;
Moreover, it was known she was
Her wealthy father's heir!

Now when the Injuns saw that band
They trembled with affright,
And yet they thought the cheapest thing
To do was stay and fight.

So sturdily they stood their ground,
Nor would their prisoner yield,
Despite the wrath of Willie Clow
And gallant Dady Field.

Oh, never fiercer battle raged
Upon the Waller Lot,
And never blood more freely flowed
Than flowed for Sissy Knott!

An Injun chief of monstrous size
Got Kendall Evans down,
And Robbie James was soon o'erthrown
By one of great renown.

And Dady Field was sorely done,
And Willie Clow was hurt,
And all that gallant cow-boy band
Lay wallowing in the dirt.

But still they strove with might and main
Till all the Waller Lot
Was strewn with hair and gouts of gore—

All, all for Sissy Knott!

Then cried the maiden in despair:
"Alas, I sadly fear
The battle and my hopes are lost,
Unless some help appear!"

Lo, as she spoke, she saw afar
The rescuer looming up—
The pride of all Buena Park,
Clow's famous yellow pup!

"Now, sick'em, Don," the maiden cried,
"Now, sick'em, Don!" cried she;
Obedient Don at once complied—
As ordered, so did he.

He sicked'em all so passing well
That, overcome by fright,
The Indian horde gave up the fray
And safety sought in flight.

They ran and ran and ran and ran
O'er valley, plain, and hill;
And if they are not walking now,
Why, then, they're running still.

The cow-boys rose up from the dust
With faces black and blue;
"Remember, beauteous maid," said they,
"We've bled and died for you!"

"And though we suffer grievously,
We gladly hail the lot
That brings us toils and pains and wounds
For charming Sissy Knott!"

But Sissy Knott still wailed and wept,
And still her fate reviled;
For who could patch her dolly up—
Who, who could mend her child?

Then out her doting mother came,
And soothed her daughter then;
"Grieve not, my darling, I will sew
Your dolly up again!"

Joy soon succeeded unto grief,
And tears were soon dried up,
And dignities were heaped upon
Clow's noble yellow pup.

Him all that goodly company
Did as deliverer hail—
They tied a ribbon round his neck,
Another round his tail.

And every anniversary day
Upon the Waller Lot
They celebrate the victory won
For charming Sissy Knott.

And I, the poet of these folk,
Am ordered to compile
This truly famous history
In good old ballad style.

Which having done as to have earned
The sweet rewards of fame,
In what same style I did begin
I now shall end the same.

So let us sing: Long live the King,
Long live the Queen and Jack,
Long live the ten-spot and the ace,
And also all the pack.

THE STORK

Last night the Stork came stalking,
And, Stork, beneath your wing
Lay, lapped in dreamless slumber,
The tiniest little thing!
From Babyland, out yonder
Beside a silver sea,
You brought a priceless treasure
As gift to mine and me!

Last night my dear one listened—
And, wife, you knew the cry—
The dear old Stork has sought our home
A many times gone by!
And in your gentle bosom
I found the pretty thing
That from the realm out yonder
Our friend the Stork did bring.

Last night a babe awakened,
And, babe, how strange and new
Must seem the home and people

The Stork has brought you to;
And yet methinks you like them—
You neither stare nor weep,
But closer to my dear one
You cuddle, and you sleep!

Last night my heart grew fonder—
O happy heart of mine,
Sing of the inspirations
That round my pathway shine!
And sing your sweetest love-song
To this dear nestling wee
The Stork from 'Way-Out-Yonder
Hath brought to mine and me!

THE BOTTLE TREE

A bottle tree bloometh in Winkyway land—
Heigh-ho for a bottle, I say!
A snug little berth in that ship I demand
That rocketh the Bottle-Tree babies away
Where the Bottle Tree bloometh by night and by day
And reacheth its fruit to each wee, dimpled hand;
You take of that fruit as much as you list,
For colic's a nuisance that doesn't exist!
So cuddle me and cuddle me fast,
And cuddle me snug in my cradle away,
For I hunger and thirst for that precious repast—
Heigh-ho for a bottle, I say!

The Bottle Tree bloometh by night and by day!
Heigh-ho for Winkyway land!
And Bottle-Tree fruit (as I've heard people say)
Makes bellies of Bottle-Tree babies expand—
And that is a trick I would fain understand!
Heigh-ho for a bottle to-day!
And heigh-ho for a bottle to-night—
A bottle of milk that is creamy and white!
So cuddle me close, and cuddle me fast,
And cuddle me snug in my cradle away,
For I hunger and thirst for that precious repast—
Heigh-ho for a bottle, I say!

GOOGLY-GOO

Of mornings, bright and early,
When the lark is on the wing

And the robin in the maple
Hops from her nest to sing,
From yonder cheery chamber
Cometh a mellow coo—
'T is the sweet, persuasive treble
Of my little Googly-Goo!

The sunbeams hear his music,
And they seek his little bed,
And they dance their prettiest dances
Round his golden curly head:
Schottisches, galops, minuets,
Gavottes and waltzes, too,
Dance they unto the music
Of my googling Googly-Goo.

My heart—my heart it leapeth
To hear that treble tone;
What music like thy music,
My darling and mine own!
And patiently—yes, cheerfully
I toil the long day through—
My labor seemeth lightened
By the song of Googly-Goo!

I may not see his antics,
Nor kiss his dimpled cheek:
I may not smooth the tresses
The sunbeams love to seek;
It mattereth not—the echo
Of his sweet, persuasive coo
Recurreth to remind me
Of my little Googly-Goo.

And when I come at evening,
I stand without the door
And patiently I listen
For that dear sound once more;
And oftentimes I wonder,
"Oh, God! what should I do
If any ill should happen
To my little Googly-Goo!"

Then in affright I call him—
I hear his gleeful shouts!
Begone, ye dread forebodings—
Begone, ye killing doubts!
For, with my arms about him,
My heart warms through and through
With the oogling and the googling
Of my little Googly-Goo!

THE BENCH-LEGGED FYCE

Speakin' of dorgs, my bench-legged fyce
Hed most o' the virtues, an' nary a vice.
Some folks called him Sooner, a name that arose
From his predisposition to chronic repose;
But, rouse his ambition, he couldn't be beat—
Yer bet yer he got thar on all his four feet!

Mos' dorgs hez some forte—like huntin' an' such,
But the sports o' the field didn't bother him much;
Wuz just a plain dorg, an' contented to be
On peaceable terms with the neighbors an' me;
Used to fiddle an' squirm, and grunt "Oh, how nice!"
When I tickled the back of that bench-legged fyce!

He wuz long in the bar'l, like a fyce oughter be;
His color wuz yaller as ever you see;
His tail, curlin' upward, wuz long, loose, an' slim—
When he didn't wag it, why, the tail it wagged him!
His legs wuz so crooked, my bench-legged pup
Wuz as tall settin' down as he wuz standin' up!

He'd lie by the stove of a night an' regret
The various vittles an' things he had et;
When a stranger, most likely a tramp, come along,
He'd lift up his voice in significant song—
You wondered, by gum! how there ever wuz space
In that bosom o' his'n to hold so much bass!

Of daytimes he'd sneak to the road an' lie down,
An' tackle the country dorgs comin' to town;
By common consent he wuz boss in St. Joe,
For what he took hold of he never let go!
An' a dude that come courtin' our girl left a slice
Of his white flannel suit with our bench-legged fyce!

He wuz good to us kids—when we pulled at his fur
Or twisted his tail he would never demur;
He seemed to enjoy all our play an' our chaff,
For his tongue 'u'd hang out an' he'd laff an' he'd laff;
An' once, when the Hobart boy fell through the ice,
He wuz drug clean ashore by that bench-legged fyce!

We all hev our choice, an' you, like the rest,
Allow that the dorg which you've got is the best;
I wouldn't give much for the boy 'at grows up
With no friendship subsistin' 'tween him an' a pup!

When a fellow gits old—I tell you it's nice
To think of his youth and his bench-legged fyce!

To think of the springtime 'way back in St. Joe—
Of the peach-trees abloom an' the daisies ablow;
To think of the play in the medder an' grove,
When little legs wrassled an' little han's strove;
To think of the loyalty, valor, an' truth
Of the friendships that hallow the season of youth!

LITTLE MISS BRAG

Little Miss Brag has much to say
To the rich little lady from over the way
And the rich little lady puts out a lip
As she looks at her own white, dainty slip,
And wishes that she could wear a gown
As pretty as gingham of faded brown!
For little Miss Brag she lays much stress
On the privileges of a gingham dress—
"Aha,
Oho!"

The rich little lady from over the way
Has beautiful dolls in vast array;
Yet she envies the raggedy home-made doll
She hears our little Miss Brag extol.
For the raggedy doll can fear no hurt
From wet, or heat, or tumble, or dirt!
Her nose is inked, and her mouth is, too,
And one eye's black and the other's blue—
"Aha,
Oho!"

The rich little lady goes out to ride
With footmen standing up outside,
Yet wishes that, sometimes, after dark
Her father would trundle her in the park;—
That, sometimes, her mother would sing the things
Little Miss Brag says her mother sings
When through the attic window streams
The moonlight full of golden dreams—
"Aha,
Oho!"

Yes, little Miss Brag has much to say
To the rich little lady from over the way;
And yet who knows but from her heart
Often the bitter sighs upstart—

Uprise to lose their burn and sting
In the grace of the tongue that loves to sing
Praise of the treasures all its own!
So I've come to love that treble tone—
"Aha,
Oho!"

THE HUMMING TOP

The top it hummeth a sweet, sweet song
To my dear little boy at play—
Merrily singeth all day long,
As it spinneth and spinneth away.
And my dear little boy
He laugheth with joy
When he heareth the monotone
Of that busy thing
That loveth to sing
The song that is all its own.

Hold fast the string and wind it tight,
That the song be loud and clear;
Now hurl the top with all your might
Upon the banquette here;
And straight from the string
The joyous thing
Boundeth and spinneth along,
And it whirrs and it chirrs
And it birrs and it purrs
Ever its pretty song.

Will ever my dear little boy grow old,
As some have grown before?
Will ever his heart feel faint and cold,
When he heareth the songs of yore?
Will ever this toy
Of my dear little boy,
When the years have worn away,
Sing sad and low
Of the long ago,
As it singeth to me to-day?

LADY BUTTON-EYES

When the busy day is done,
And my weary little one
Rocketh gently to and fro;

When the night winds softly blow,
And the crickets in the glen
Chirp and chirp and chirp again;
When upon the haunted green
Fairies dance around their queen—
Then from yonder misty skies
Cometh Lady Button-Eyes.

Through the murk and mist and gloam
To our quiet, cozy home,
Where to singing, sweet and low,
Rocks a cradle to and fro;
Where the clock's dull monotone
Telleth of the day that's done;
Where the moonbeams hover o'er
Playthings sleeping on the floor—
Where my weary wee one lies
Cometh Lady Button-Eyes.

Cometh like a fleeting ghost
From some distant eerie coast;
Never footfall can you hear
As that spirit fareth near—
Never whisper, never word
From that shadow-queen is heard.
In ethereal raiment dight,
From the realm of fay and sprite
In the depth of yonder skies
Cometh Lady Button-Eyes.

Layeth she her hands upon
My dear weary little one,
And those white hands overspread
Like a veil the curly head,
Seem to fondle and caress
Every little silken tress;
Then she smooths the eyelids down
Over those two eyes of brown—
In such soothing, tender wise
Cometh Lady Button-Eyes.

Dearest, feel upon your brow
That caressing magic now;
For the crickets in the glen
Chirp and chirp and chirp again,
While upon the haunted green
Fairies dance around their queen,
And the moonbeams hover o'er
Playthings sleeping on the floor—
Hush, my sweet! from yonder skies
Cometh Lady Button-Eyes!

Play that my knee was a calico mare
Saddled and bridled for Bumpville;
Leap to the back of this steed, if you dare,
And gallop away to Bumpville!
I hope you'll be sure to sit fast in your seat,
For this calico mare is prodigiously fleet,
And many adventures you're likely to meet
As you journey along to Bumpville.

This calico mare both gallops and trots
While whisking you off to Bumpville;
She paces, she shies, and she stumbles, in spots,
In the tortuous road to Bumpville;
And sometimes this strangely mercurial steed
Will suddenly stop and refuse to proceed,
Which, all will admit, is vexatious indeed,
When one is en route to Bumpville!

She's scared of the cars when the engine goes "Toot!"
Down by the crossing at Bumpville;
You'd better look out for that treacherous brute
Bearing you off to Bumpville!
With a snort she rears up on her hindermost heels,
And executes jigs and Virginia reels—
Words fail to explain how embarrassed one feels
Dancing so wildly to Bumpville!

It's bumpytybump and it's jiggytyjog,
Journeying on to Bumpville
It's over the hilltop and down through the bog
You ride on your way to Bumpville;
It's rattletybang over boulder and stump,
There are rivers to ford, there are fences to jump,
And the corduroy road it goes bumpytybump,
Mile after mile to bumpville!

Perhaps you'll observe it's no easy thing
Making the journey to Bumpville,
So I think, on the whole, it were prudent to bring
An end to this ride to Bumpville;
For, though she has uttered no protest or plaint,
The calico mare must be blowing and faint—
What's more to the point, I'm blowed if I ain't!
So play we have got to Bumpville!

THE BROOK

I looked in the brook and saw a face—
Heigh-ho, but a child was I!
There were rushes and willows in that place,
And they clutched at the brook as the brook ran by;
And the brook it ran its own sweet way,
As a child doth run in heedless play,
And as it ran I heard it say:
"Hasten with me
To the roistering sea
That is wroth with the flame of the morning sky!"

I look in the brook and see a face—
Heigh-ho, but the years go by!
The rushes are dead in the old-time place,
And the willows I knew when a child was I.
And the brook it seemeth to me to say,
As ever it stealeth on its way—
Solemnly now, and not in play:
"Oh, come with me
To the slumbrous sea
That is gray with the peace of the evening sky!"

Heigh-ho, but the years go by—
I would to God that a child were I!

PICNIC-TIME

It's June ag'in, an' in my soul I feel the fillin' joy
That's sure to come this time o' year to every little boy;
For, every June, the Sunday-schools at picnics may be seen,
Where "fields beyont the swellin' floods stand dressed in livin' green";
Where little girls are skeered to death with spiders, bugs, and ants,
An' little boys get grass-stains on their go-to meetin' pants.
It's June ag'in, an' with it all what happiness is mine—
There's goin' to be a picnic, an' I'm goin' to jine!

One year I jined the Baptists, an' goodness! how it rained!
(But grampa says that that's the way "baptizo" is explained.)
And once I jined the 'Piscopils an' had a heap o' fun—
But the boss of all the picnics was the Presbyteriun!
They had so many puddin's, sallids, sandwidges, an' pies,
That a feller wisht his stummick was as hungry as his eyes!
Oh, yes, the eatin' Presbyteriuns give yer is so fine
That when they have a picnic, you bet I'm goin' to jine!

But at this time the Methodists have special claims on me,

For they're goin' to give a picnic on the 21st, D. V.;
Why should a liberal universalist like me object
To share the joys of fellowship with every friendly sect?
However het'rodox their articles of faith elsewise may be,
Their doctrine of fried chick'n is a savin' grace to me!
So on the 21st of June, the weather bein' fine,
They're goin' to give a picnic, and I'm goin' to jine!

SHUFFLE-SHOON AND AMBER-LOCKS

Shuffle-shoon and Amber-Locks
Sit together, building blocks;
Shuffle-Shoon is old and gray,
Amber-Locks a little child,
But together at their play
Age and Youth are reconciled,
And with sympathetic glee
Build their castles fair to see.

"When I grow to be a man"
(So the wee one's prattle ran),
"I shall build a castle so—
With a gateway broad and grand;
Here a pretty vine shall grow,
There a soldier guard shall stand;
And the tower shall be so high,
Folks will wonder, by and by!"

Shuffle-Shoon quoth: "Yes, I know;
Thus I builded long ago!
Here a gate and there a wall,
Here a window, there a door;
Here a steeple wondrous tall
Riseth ever more and more!
But the years have leveled low
What I builded long ago!"

So they gossip at their play,
Heedless of the fleeting day;
One speaks of the Long Ago
Where his dead hopes buried lie;
One with chubby cheeks aglow
Prattleth of the By and By;
Side by side, they build their blocks—
Shuffle-Shoon and Amber-Locks.

THE SHUT-EYE TRAIN

Come, my little one, with me!
There are wondrous sights to see
As the evening shadows fall;
In your pretty cap and gown,
Don't detain
The Shut-Eye train—
"Ting-a-ling!" the bell it goeth,
"Toot-toot!" the whistle bloweth,
And we hear the warning call:
"All aboard for Shut-Eye Town!"

Over hill and over plain
Soon will speed the Shut-Eye train!
Through the blue where bloom the stars
And the Mother Moon looks down
We'll away
To land of Fay—
Oh, the sights that we shall see there!
Come, my little one, with me there—
'T is a goodly train of cars—
All aboard for Shut-Eye Town!

Swifter than a wild bird's flight,
Through the realms of fleecy light
We shall speed and speed away!
Let the Night in envy frown—
What care we
How wroth she be!
To the Balow-land above us,
To the Balow-folk who love us,
Let us hasten while we may—
All aboard for Shut-Eye Town!

Shut-Eye Town is passing fair—
Golden dreams await us there;
We shall dream those dreams, my dear,
Till the Mother Moon goes down—
See unfold
Delights untold!
And in those mysterious places
We shall see beloved faces
And beloved voices hear
In the grace of Shut-Eye Town.

Heavy are your eyes, my sweet,
Weary are your little feet—
Nestle closer up to me
In your pretty cap and gown;
Don't detain
The Shut-Eye train!

"Ting-a-ling!" the bell it goeth,
"Toot-toot!" the whistle bloweth
Oh, the sights that we shall see!
All aboard for Shut-Eye Town!

LITTLE—OH DEAR

See, what a wonderful garden is here,
Planted and trimmed for my Little-Oh-Dear!
Posies so gaudy and grass of such brown—
Search ye the country and hunt ye the town
And never ye'll meet with a garden so queer
As this one I've made for my Little-Oh-Dear!

Marigolds white and buttercups blue,
Lilies all dabbled with honey and dew,
The cactus that trails over trellis and wall,
Roses and pansies and violets—all
Make proper obeisance and reverent cheer
When into her garden steps Little-Oh-Dear.

And up at the top of that lavender-tree
A silver-bird singeth as only can she;
For, ever and only, she singeth the song
"I love you—I love you!" the happy day long;—
Then the echo—the echo that smiteth me here!
"I love you, I love you," my Little-Oh-Dear!

The garden may wither, the silver-bird fly—
But what careth my little precious, or I?
From her pathway of flowers that in spring time upstart
She walketh the tenderer way in my heart
And, oh, it is always the summer-time here
With that song of "I love you," my Little-Oh-Dear!

THE FLY-AWAY HORSE

Oh, a wonderful horse is the Fly-Away Horse—
Perhaps you have seen him before;
Perhaps, while you slept, his shadow has swept
Through the moonlight that floats on the floor.
For it's only at night, when the stars twinkle bright,
That the Fly-Away Horse, with a neigh
And a pull at his rein and a toss of his mane,
Is up on his heels and away!
The Moon in the sky,
As he gallopeth by,

Cries: "Oh! what a marvelous sight!"
And the Stars in dismay
Hide their faces away
In the lap of old Grandmother Night.

It is yonder, out yonder, the Fly-Away Horse
Speedeth ever and ever away—
Over meadows and lanes, over mountains and plains,
Over streamlets that sing at their play;
And over the sea like a ghost sweepeth he,
While the ships they go sailing below,
And he speedeth so fast that the men at the mast
Adjudge him some portent of woe.
"What ho there!" they cry,
As he flourishes by
With a whisk of his beautiful tail;
And the fish in the sea
Are as scared as can be,
From the nautilus up to the whale!

And the Fly-Away Horse seeks those faraway lands
You little folk dream of at night—
Where candy-trees grow, and honey-brooks flow,
And corn-fields with popcorn are white;
And the beasts in the wood are ever so good
To children who visit them there—
What glory astride of a lion to ride,
Or to wrestle around with a bear!
The monkeys, they say:
"Come on, let us play,"
And they frisk in the cocoanut-trees:
While the parrots, that cling
To the peanut-vines, sing
Or converse with comparative ease!

Off! scamper to bed—you shall ride him tonight!
For, as soon as you've fallen asleep,
With a jubilant neigh he shall bear you away
Over forest and hillside and deep!
But tell us, my dear, all you see and you hear
In those beautiful lands over there,
Where the Fly-Away Horse wings his faraway course
With the wee one consigned to his care.
Then grandma will cry
In amazement: "Oh, my!"
And she'll think it could never be so;
And only we two
Shall know it is true—
You and I, little precious! shall know!

SWING HIGH AND SWING LOW

Swing high and swing low
While the breezes they blow—
It's off for a sailor thy father would go;
And it's here in the harbor, in sight of the sea,
He hath left his wee babe with my song and with me:
"Swing high and swing low
While the breezes they blow!"

Swing high and swing low
While the breezes they blow—
It's oh for the waiting as weary days go!
And it's oh for the heartache that smiteth me when
I sing my song over and over again:
"Swing high and swing low
While the breezes they blow!"

"Swing high and swing low "—
The sea singeth so,
And it waileth anon in its ebb and its flow;
And a sleeper sleeps on to that song of the sea
Nor recketh he ever of mine or of me!
"Swing high and swing low
While the breezes they blow—
'T was off for a sailor thy father would go!"

WHEN I WAS A BOY

Up in the attic where I slept
When I was a boy, a little boy,
In through the lattice the moonlight crept,
Bringing a tide of dreams that swept
Over the low, red trundle-bed,
Bathing the tangled curly head,
While moonbeams played at hide-and-seek
With the dimples on the sun-browned cheek—
When I was a boy, a little boy!

And, oh! the dreams—the dreams I dreamed!
When I was a boy, a little boy!
For the grace that through the lattice streamed
Over my folded eyelids seemed
To have the gift of prophecy,
And to bring me glimpses of times to be
When manhood's clarion seemed to call—
Ah! that was the sweetest dream of all,
When I was a boy, a little boy!

I'd like to sleep where I used to sleep
When I was a boy, a little boy!
For in at the lattice the moon would peep,
Bringing her tide of dreams to sweep
The crosses and griefs of the years away
From the heart that is weary and faint to-day;
And those dreams should give me back again
A peace I have never known since then—
When I was a boy, a little boy!

AT PLAY

Play that you are mother dear,
And play that papa is your beau;
Play that we sit in the corner here,
Just as we used to, long ago.
Playing so, we lovers two
Are just as happy as we can be,
And I'll say "I love you" to you,
And you say "I love you" to me!
"I love you" we both shall say,
All in earnest and all in play.

Or, play that you are that other one
That some time came, and went away;
And play that the light of years agone
Stole into my heart again to-day!
Playing that you are the one I knew
In the days that never again may be,
I'll say "I love you" to you,"
And you say "I love you" to me!
"I love you!" my heart shall say
To the ghost of the past come back to-day!

Or, play that you sought this nestling-place
For your own sweet self, with that dual guise
Of your pretty mother in your face
And the look of that other in your eyes!
So the dear old loves shall live anew
As I hold my darling on my knee,
And I'll say "I love you" to you,
And you say "I love you" to me!
Oh, many a strange, true thing we say
And do when we pretend to play!

A VALENTINE

Go, Cupid, and my sweetheart tell
I love her well.
Yes, though she tramples on my heart
And rends that bleeding thing apart;
And though she rolls a scornful eye
On doting me when I go by;
And though she scouts at everything
As tribute unto her I bring—
Apple, banana, caramel—
Haste, Cupid, to my love and tell,
In spite of all, I love her well!

And further say I have a sled
Cushioned in blue and painted red!
The groceryman has promised I
Can "hitch" whenever he goes by—
Go, tell her that, and, furthermore,
Apprise my sweetheart that a score
Of other little girls implore
The boon of riding on that sled
Painted and hitched, as aforesaid;—
And tell her, Cupid, only she
Shall ride upon that sled with me!
Tell her this all, and further tell
I love her well.

LITTLE ALL-ALONEY

Little All-Aloney's feet
Pitter-patter in the hall,
And his mother runs to meet
And to kiss her toddling sweet,
Ere perchance he fall.
He is, oh, so weak and small!
Yet what danger shall he fear
When his mother hovereth near,
And he hears her cheering call:
"All-Aloney"?

Little All-Aloney's face
It is all aglow with glee,
As around that romping-place
At a terrifying pace
Lungeth, plungeth he!
And that hero seems to be
All unconscious of our cheers—
Only one dear voice he hears
Calling reassuringly:

"All-Aloney!"

Though his legs bend with their load,
Though his feet they seem so small
That you cannot help forebode
Some disastrous episode
In that noisy hall,
Neither threatening bump nor fall
Little All-Aloney fears,
But with sweet bravado steers
Whither comes that cheery call:
"All-Aloney!"

Ah, that in the years to come,
When he shares of Sorrow's store,—
When his feet are chill and numb,
When his cross is burdensome,
And his heart is sore:
Would that he could hear once more
The gentle voice he used to hear—
Divine with mother love and cheer—
Calling from yonder spirit shore:
"All, all alone!"

SEEIN' THINGS

I ain't afeard uv snakes, or toads, or bugs, or worms, or mice,
An' things 'at girls are skeered uv I think are awful nice!
I'm pretty brave, I guess; an' yet I hate to go to bed,
For, when I'm tucked up warm an' snug an' when my prayers are said,
Mother tells me "Happy dreams!" and takes away the light,
An' leaves me lyin' all alone an' seein' things at night!

Sometimes they're in the corner, sometimes they're by the door,
Sometimes they're all a-standin' in the middle uv the floor;
Sometimes they are a-sittin' down, sometimes they're walkin' round
So softly an' so creepylike they never make a sound!
Sometimes they are as black as ink, an' other times they're white—
But the color ain't no difference when you see things at night!

Once, when I licked a feller 'at had just moved on our street,
An' father sent me up to bed without a bite to eat,
I woke up in the dark an' saw things standin' in a row,
A-lookin' at me cross-eyed an' p'intin' at me—so!
Oh, my! I wuz so skeered that time I never slep' a mite—
It's almost alluz when I'm bad I see things at night!

Lucky thing I ain't a girl, or I'd be skeered to death!
Bein' I'm a boy, I duck my head an' hold my breath;

An' I am, oh! so sorry I'm a naughty boy, an' then
I promise to be better an' I say my prayers again!
Gran'ma tells me that's the only way to make it right
When a feller has been wicked an' sees things at night!
An' so, when other naughty boys would coax me into sin,
I try to skwush the Tempter's voice 'at urges me within;
An' when they's pie for supper, or cakes 'at 's big an' nice,
I want to—but I do not pass my plate f'r them things twice!
No, ruther let Starvation wipe me slowly out o' sight
Than I should keep a-livin' on an' seein' things at night!

THE CUNNIN' LITTLE THING

When baby wakes of mornings,
Then it's wake, ye people all!
For another day
Of song and play
Has come at our darling's call!
And, till she gets her dinner,
She makes the welkin ring,
And she won't keep still till she's had her fill—
The cunnin' little thing!

When baby goes a-walking,
Oh, how her paddies fly!
For that's the way
The babies say
To other folk "by-by";
The trees bend down to kiss her,
And the birds in rapture sing,
As there she stands and waves her hands—
The cunnin' little thing!

When baby goes a-rocking
In her bed at close of day,
At hide-and-seek
On her dainty cheek
The dreams and the dimples play;
Then it's sleep in the tender kisses
The guardian angels bring
From the Far Above to my sweetest love—
You cunnin' little thing!

THE DOLL'S WOOING

The little French doll was a dear little doll
Tricked out in the sweetest of dresses;

Her eyes were of hue
A most delicate blue
And dark as the night were her tresses;
Her dear little mouth was fluted and red,
And this little French doll was so very well bred
That whenever accosted her little mouth said
"Mamma! mamma!"

The stockinet doll, with one arm and one leg,
Had once been a handsome young fellow;
But now he appeared
Rather frowzy and bleared
In his torn regimentals of yellow;
Yet his heart gave a curious thump as he lay
In the little toy cart near the window one day
And heard the sweet voice of that French dolly say:
"Mamma! mamma!"

He listened so long and he listened so hard
That anon he grew ever so tender,
For it's everywhere known
That the feminine tone
Gets away with all masculine gender!
He up and he wooed her with soldierly zest
But all she'd reply to the love he professed
Were these plaintive words (which perhaps you have guessed):
"Mamma! mamma!"

Her mother—a sweet little lady of five—
Vouchsafed her parental protection,
And although stockinet
Wasn't blue-blooded, yet
She really could make no objection!
So soldier and dolly were wedded one day,
And a moment ago, as I journeyed that way,
I'm sure that I heard a wee baby voice say:
"Mamma! mamma!"

INSCRIPTION FOR MY LITTLE SON'S SILVER PLATE

When thou dost eat from off this plate,
I charge thee be thou temperate;
Unto thine elders at the board
Do thou sweet reverence accord;
And, though to dignity inclined,
Unto the serving-folk be kind;
Be ever mindful of the poor,
Nor turn them hungry from the door;
And unto God, for health and food

And all that in thy life is good,
Give thou thy heart in gratitude.

FISHERMAN JIM'S KIDS

Fisherman Jim lived on the hill
With his bonnie wife an' his little boys;
'T wuz "Blow, ye winds, as blow ye will—
Naught we reck of your cold and noise!"
For happy and warm were he an' his,
And he dandled his kids upon his knee
To the song of the sea.

Fisherman Jim would sail all day,
But, when come night, upon the sands
His little kids ran from their play,
Callin' to him an' wavin' their hands;
Though the wind was fresh and the sea was high,
He'd hear 'em—you bet—above the roar
Of the waves on the shore!

Once Fisherman Jim sailed into the bay
As the sun went down in a cloudy sky,
And never a kid saw he at play,
And he listened in vain for the welcoming cry.
In his little house he learned it all,
And he clinched his hands and he bowed his head—
"The fever!" they said.

'T wuz a pitiful time for Fisherman Jim,
With them darlin's a-dyin' afore his eyes,
A-stretchin' their wee hands out to him
An' a-breakin' his heart with the old-time cries
He had heerd so often upon the sands;
For they thought they wuz helpin' his boat ashore—
Till they spoke no more.

But Fisherman Jim lived on and on,
Castin' his nets an' sailin' the sea;
As a man will live when his heart is gone,
Fisherman Jim lived hopelessly,
Till once in those years they come an' said:
"Old Fisherman Jim is powerful sick—
Go to him, quick!"

Then Fisherman Jim says he to me:
"It's a long, long cruise-you understand—
But over beyont the ragin' sea
I kin see my boys on the shinin' sand

Waitin' to help this ol' hulk ashore,
Just as they used to—ah, mate, you know!—
In the long ago."

No, sir! he wuzn't afeard to die;
For all night long he seemed to see
His little boys of the days gone by,
An' to hear sweet voices forgot by me!
An' just as the mornin' sun come up—
"They're holdin' me by the hands!" he cried,
An' so he died.

"FIDDLE-DEE-DEE"

There once was a bird that lived up in a tree,
And all he could whistle was "Fiddle-dee-dee"—
A very provoking, unmusical song
For one to be whistling the summer day long!
Yet always contented and busy was he
With that vocal recurrence of "Fiddle-dee-dee."

Hard by lived a brave little soldier of four,
That weird iteration repented him sore;
"I prithee, Dear-Mother-Mine! fetch me my gun,
For, by our St. Didy! the deed must be done
That shall presently rid all creation and me
Of that ominous bird and his 'Fiddle-dee-dee'!"

Then out came Dear-Mother-Mine, bringing her son
His awfully truculent little red gun;
The stock was of pine and the barrel of tin,
The "bang" it came out where the bullet went in—
The right kind of weapon I think you'll agree
For slaying all fowl that go "Fiddle-dee-dee"!

The brave little soldier quoth never a word,
But he up and he drew a straight bead on that bird;
And, while that vain creature provokingly sang,
The gun it went off with a terrible bang!
Then loud laughed the youth—"By my Bottle," cried he,
"I've put a quietus on 'Fiddle-dee-dee'!"

Out came then Dear-Mother-Mine, saying: "My son,
Right well have you wrought with your little red gun!
Hereafter no evil at all need I fear,
With such a brave soldier as You-My-Love here!"
She kissed the dear boy.
(The bird in the tree
Continued to whistle his "Fiddle-dee-dee")

Over the hills and far away,
A little boy steals from his morning play
And under the blossoming apple-tree
He lies and he dreams of the things to be:
Of battles fought and of victories won,
Of wrongs o'erthrown and of great deeds done—
Of the valor that he shall prove some day,
Over the hills and far away—
Over the hills, and far away!

Over the hills and far away
It's, oh, for the toil the livelong day!
But it mattereth not to the soul aflame
With a love for riches and power and fame!
On, O man! while the sun is high—
On to the certain joys that lie
Yonder where blazeth the noon of day,
Over the hills and far away—
Over the hills, and far away!

Over the hills and far away,
An old man lingers at close of day;
Now that his journey is almost done,
His battles fought and his victories won—
The old-time honesty and truth,
The trustfulness and the friends of youth,
Home and mother-where are they?
Over the hills and far away—
Over the years, and far away!

Eugene Field – A Short Biography

Eugene Field was born on 2nd September, 1850 in St. Louis, Missouri at 634 S. Broadway to parents Roswell Martin and Frances Reed Field, both of New England stock. Tragically Field lost his mother at age 6 and was thereafter brought up by a cousin, Mary Field French, in Amherst, Massachusetts.

Field attended Williams College in Williamstown, Massachusetts.

When he was 19 his father died, and Field dropped out of Williams. Field's father, Roswell Martin Field, was the lawyer for Dred Scott, the slave who famously sued for his freedom. The complaint was sometimes referred to as 'The lawsuit that started the Civil War'.

Field then went to Knox College in Galesburg, Illinois, but again dropped out. This time after a year. However he did then summon himself to attend the University of Missouri in Columbia, Missouri, where his brother Roswell was studying. As can be gathered from his efforts to date Field was not the most serious of students but was gaining the reputation of being a prankster. Among his more outlandish attempts were a raid on the president's wine cellar, painting the president's house in school colors, and firing the school's landmark cannons at midnight.

Field tried acting but found it not to his liking, studied law but with little success, but did have an interest in writing for the student newspaper.

When his studies finished in 1871, although he never graduated, he collected his share of his inheritance from his father's estate, and set off for a trip to explore Europe. After six months, with funds from the inheritance exhausted, he returned to the United States.

Field then set to work as a journalist for the St. Joseph Gazette in Saint Joseph, Missouri, in 1875.

That same year he married the sixteen-year-old Julia Sutherland Comstock of St Joseph, Missouri. They would eventually have eight children during their twenty-two years of marriage, of whom only five would reach adulthood. Field, knowing that his understanding of finances was somewhat poor, arranged for all the money he earned to be sent to his wife for her to administer on behalf of the family.

In his career as a journalist he soon found a niche that suited him. His articles were light, humorous and written in a personal and gossipy style that endeared him to his readership. Some were soon being syndicated to other newspapers around the States. Field rose to be the city editor of the Gazette.

From 1876 through 1880, the Family lived in St. Louis. Field worked initially as an editorial writer for the Morning Journal and then for the Times-Journal. From there he worked for a short time as the managing editor of the Kansas City Times before settling, for two years, as the editor of the Denver Tribune. He also wrote a column for the paper, 'Odds and Ends,' poking fun at the climate, the muddy roads, the frontier language, and other aspects of Denver life. However his readership was large and growing. Further opportunities would come.

In 1883 the Field moved the family to Chicago lured by a salary of $50 a week. Field now began work for the Chicago Daily News. Here he wrote his humorous newspaper column called Sharps and Flats. He quickly found out that $50 dollars in Denver didn't stretch that far in bustling Chicago.

His column ran in the newspaper's morning edition. In it Field made quips about issues and personalities of the day, especially regarding the arts and literature. His pet subject was the intellectual superiority of Chicago, especially when he compared it to Boston, which he often did. In April 1887, he wrote, "While Chicago is humping herself in the interests of literature, art and the sciences, vain old Boston is frivoling away her precious time in an attempted renaissance of the cod fisheries."

In another article that year after Chicago's National League baseball club sold future baseball Hall of Famer Mike "King" Kelly to Boston which overlapped with a speaking tour visit from the famous Boston poet and diplomat James Russell Lowell he wrote: "Chicago feels a special interest in Mr. Lowell at this particular time because he is perhaps the foremost representative of the enterprising and opulent community which within the last week has secured the services of one of Chicago's honored sons for the base-ball season of 1887. The fact that Boston has come to Chicago for the captain of her baseball nine has reinvigorated the bonds of affection between the metropolis of the

Bay state and the metropolis of the mighty west; the truth of this will appear in the mighty welcome which our public will give Mr. Lowell next Tuesday."

It was in 1888 that his poem 'Little Boy Blue' was printed in America, a weekly journal. It achieved for Field instant and lasting fame. Coincidentally the same issue carried a poem by James Russell Lowell. Field was immensely pleased that his own poem was regarded with considerably more weight and acclaim.

Field had first published poetry in 1879, when his poem 'Christmas Treasures' was published. It later appeared in 'A Little Book of Western Verse' (1889). This was the beginning that would eventually number over a dozen volumes. He developed a style of light-hearted poems for children. Among the perennial favorites are 'Wynken, Blynken, and Nod' and 'The Duel' (but better known as 'The Gingham Dog and the Calico Cat') and 'Little Boy Blue' about the death of a child. As well as verse Field published an extensive range of short stories including 'The Holy Cross' and 'Daniel and the Devil.'

Field treasured rare, unusual and beautiful books and his personal library had scores of them. He also enjoyed making them too and frequently worked long hours with great care and various colored inks decorating the first letter of his poems.

In 1889 whilst the family were in London and Field himself was recovering from a bout of ill health he wrote his most famous poem; 'Lovers Lane'. It is often thought to have been written whilst the couple were courting but recent research settles it authorship to this later date. The poem was written as a reminder of better days when the couple courted in her father's buggy on 'Lover's Lane, St Jo'.

Field was ever curious and keen to push his boundaries. In 1891 with his brother Roswell they wrote and published 'Echoes from the Sabine Farm' a loosely translated version of Horace.

On 4th November 1895 Eugene Field Sr died in Chicago of a heart attack at the age of 45. He is buried at the Church of the Holy Comforter in Kenilworth, Illinois.

The New York Times described his death: CHICAGO, Nov. 4. — Eugene Field, the poet and humorist, died at 5 o'clock this morning of heart disease at his residence in Buena Park. Although Mr. Field had been ill for the past three days, his sudden death was totally unexpected.

Field was originally interred at Graceland Cemetery in Chicago, but his son-in-law, Senior Warden of the Church of the Holy Comforter, had him reinterred on 7th March, 1926.

Several of his poems were set to music with commercial success. Many of his works were accompanied by paintings from the exceptional talents of Maxfield Parrish.

During his lifetime he was often referred to as the 'poet of childhood'. This may account for his anonymous publication of 'Only a Boy'. In our own times the work would probably be frowned upon. It concerns a 12-year-old boy being seduced by a woman in her 30s. The 1920's drama critic/magazine editor George Jean Nathan claimed it was a popular but forbidden work among those coming of age in the early 1900's.

Much of what Field wrote was light, humourous and of its time. And that is perhaps why it has endured. Its writes of a time that, in his words, suspends itself from the harsh reality of real life to a gentler and more touching time that exists in the imagination.

The Tribune Primer (1882)
Culture's Garland (1887)
A Little Book of Profitable Tales (1889)
A Little Book of Western Verse (1889)
With Trumpet and Drum (1892)
Echoes from the Sabine Farm (1893)
The Holy Cross and Other Tales (1893)
Second Book of Verse (1893)
Love Songs of Childhood (1894)
Love Affairs of a Bibliomaniac (1895)
Little Willie (1895)
Songs and Other Verse (1896)
Second Book of Tales (1896)
The House; An Episode in the Lives of Reuben Baker, Astronomer and His Wife Alice (1896)
Field Flowers (1896)
Florence Bardsley's Story (1897)
Lullaby Songs of Childhood (1897)
Lullaby Land (1898)
Sharps and Flats (1900)
The Stars (1901)
Nonsense for Old and Young (1901)
A Little Book of Nonsense (1901)
A Little Book of Tribune Verse (1901)
The Sabine Farm (1903)
John Smith USA (1905)
The Clink of Ice (1905)
Hoosier Lyrics (1905)
Cradle Lullabies (1909)
The Poems of Eugene Field (1910)
Christmas Tales and Christmas Verse (1912)
Penn-Yan Bill's Wooing (1914)
The Yankee Abroad (1917)
The Mouse and the Moonbeam (1919)
Poems of Childhood (1920)
The Gingham Dog and the Calico Cat (1926)
Child Verses (1927)
The Sugar Plum Tree (1929)
In Wink-a-way Land (1930)

www.ingramcontent.com/pod-product-compliance
Lightning Source LLC
Chambersburg PA
CBHW060101050426
42448CB00011B/2563